Healing Wounds

Chris Keating

BookLeaf
Publishing

Presentation by *BookLeaf Publishing*

Web: www.bookleafpub.com

E-mail: info@bookleafpub.com

ISBN: 9789395026765

First edition 2022

Healing Hurts

Healing is hard, bitter and bloody,
But it was always look so muddy.
Healing may hurt, but only for a season,
Someday you'll understand the reason.
Today hurts like hell, and it wont let down,
It feels like youre stuck and going to drown.
But I promise you this, though it's hard to
believe,
One day, and soon, you'll feel that reprieve.
Today it hurts and probably tomorrow,
But soon you'll cast away that sorrow.
Somedays are hard and others better,
But once you heal you'll remove that fetter.
No longer will you suffer in defeat,
Victory and peace you will soon greet.
Hang on for dear life, my friend.
This doesnt have to be the end.
Cry and weep and get through this night,
For we are healed by His might.

Speechless

Silence.
Something I've known too well.
Afraid to speak
Or I might be judged.
Afraid to say what I think
Because others may disagree.
Scared to say what's on my mind
Because then they'll really know.
And so I suffer in silence,
Never letting on
To what's really going on.
Others hurt worse than me
So how could i compete?
Silence is golden
No one gets hurt
Except me.
I hurt.
And I can't find the words
To tell you the pain
The raging storm inside
That suffocates me every day
That holds me tight,
Bruising me.
But you can't see those scars.
You can't see the pain

You can't see me choking back the tears
Or how I yell for help.
But all you hear is silence.
All you see is someone who is doing "fine."
But I'll sit here in silence,
Because I've lost my voice.

Hiding in Plain Sight

You get good at hiding it.
That feeling of lonliness and misery.
When you feel like a burden and so unloved,
But you can't tell anyone how you really feel.
Because in reality, they'll never understand, and
they'll never look at you the same way again.
So you bury it deep down,
and cover it up with smiles and laughter
and a face full of imitation bravery.
To all the world you seem happy and delighted,
but in reality you can't stop these feelings
of worthlessness and sorrow.
And you cant stand to hear
one more cliche to just feel better,
so you hide it away,
hoping no one will find it or uncover it.
You build walls around your heart to protect it,
not letting anyone see your vulnerability.
You get good at hiding it.
And no one knows
how much energy it takes
to act as though everything is fine,
and they wonder why you sleep so much.
But the constant battle inside
wears you out,

and you fall into a deep slumber when you
finally get home
and can be yourself.
The missed calls and canceled plans
might give you away,
but you always find an excuse
of why you couldn't make it,
but you'll catch them next time.
When in reality you just dont have it in you
to watch people celebrate
when all you want to do is cry.
You get good at hiding it.
That feeling of desolation and despair.
So you put on a face
and you always say you're fine,
but when no one is around,
those feelings come pouring out.

The Walls Around My Heart

Look at the rose.
A flower of beauty and poise.
But even it guards itself with thorns that'll cut
anyone that gets too close to defile its beauty.
And so I learned to guard my inner most beauty
with walls to keep out those that wished to harm
my inner child.
But those walls were not impervious, and the
anguish of the world seeped in, and corrupted
my inner light, nearly extinguishing it for good.
Those walls did keep some out,
distancing myself from those that wished
blessings upon me.
I guarded myself with thorns that pricked those
that got too close, causing harm to people who
only wished to bring peace.
While trying to protect myself, I caused the very
thing I tried to prevent from happening to me.
And so the petals of my own rose began to fall
off, losing myself piece by piece, till only the
stem of my existence was left.
My beauty had fallen and wilted as I tried to
protect it from being wilted with disdain, leaving
only a reminder of that affliction I caused and
endured.

Why

As I looked up into the nigh time sky,
I asked myself a simple question: why?
Why was I put here, in the endless turmoil,
Only to, one day, decay back into the soil?
Why was I the one born and not another?
Why did I exist, just like my favorite color?
The meaning of life, as I kndw it to be,
Didnt make much sense, you see.
I couldnt understand, and I couldnt fathom,
The endless void in my life, or was it a chasm?
I thought I had once discovered my reason,
But it only lasted for a tiny, short bitter season.
In the end I must say, there is one thing I know,
That life for me, just did not seem to flow.

And so I ask myself the same question,
Why was I here? But I have a suggestion.
Perhaps it was to love and give it my all,
But perhaps it was also to stumble and fall.
Life was never easy or grand,
Life's not a beach with you feet in the sand.
There's one thing for sure that I must say,
Life cannot always be like it is today.

Silence

Silence
No one knows your pain
Or the burden you bare
You keep it quiet
So they dont judge or laugh
And so they dont ask
Silence
It usually brings peace
But you scream inside
And havent known peace for awhile
But no one knows the war
That rages deep inside
Because they wouldnt understand
And would they really care
So you keep it hushed
And only whisper about your pain
Silence
It grows like a weed
Deeply rooted in the ground
And you pull it daily
So one can see
The pain you endore
In the silent hell you know
Silence
You think its gone

When you cant hear its call
But deep underground
Its roots tangle you so
Keeping you in its grasp
You keep silent
And then one day
When you try to scream
No one can hear you

Shine Bright

I'll stand aside and let you shine.
I'll stand aside, i'll be just fine.
I'll stand back so people can see your light.
Let them watch as you take flight.
Don't mind me, i've never liked the attention,
But there is just one thing i should mention.
Shine bright for all the world to see,
But please just don't forget about me.
I really don't mind staying in the back,
But i just don't want to fall through the crack.
I've always been tucked away in the shadows,
But dont forget me i must impose.
I have something to give, its a secret I've saved.
I fought some battles so the road was paved.
I dont want you to suffer the way I did,
So I gladly stepped back and so I hid.
One day you'll hear me and see my own light,
But for now, my friend, you dont have to fight.
So for now shine bright, brighter than the sun,
For soon my time being hidden soon will be done.

Chameleon

Everyone seems to belong somewhere; everyone
that is, except me.
Born in a world that has nowhere for me,
I wander alone till I find my missing piece.
No matter how much I tried to fit in,
I never fit quite right.
Always out of place and always mishapen,
I was that puzzle peice that never knew
where it fit and got lost under the couch,
forgotten to all.
Even an alien, although not belonging to this
world,
had a place where it belonged.
So why was I out of place?
Why could I never find somewhere that I
belonged?
I tried to change to fit my surroundings as a
chamleon does to blend in.
But I always stood out, like a beacon of dispair,
always different and but never unaware.
No one ever quite understood what I was,
and to be honest, I never understood either.
I didnt belong and I fear I never will.
But I guess it's not all that bad.

The misfits never fit in but they always made an
impact.
And so I go on, in my mishapen destiny,
to leave a trail behind of beauty and
contrast as I trudge forward through.

The Battle is Not Yours

Look in the mirror, and what do I see?
A stranger looking back at me.
A reflection of someone I never knew,
Because I was too busy going through.
I forgot who I was and called to be,
Because I was too busy hating me.
Those late nights crying and my darkest days,
Stopped me from believing in the One who
stays.
I looked in the mirror and no longer knew,
The person looking back had been going
through.
His eyes were swelled from the constant crying,
His eyes could show that his spirit was dying.
His head drooped down in sadness and defeat,
Because he had stopped and tried to retreat.
He no longer could fight this battle at hand,
But little did he know about the promised land.
Surely the promises fortold by the Word,
He thought werent for him, but that was absurd.
This battle he fought was no longer his own,
For soon he knew through this, he'd grown.
The man in the mirror was a reflection of past,
Because this season was never meant to last.
Now he knew who God had made him to be,

So now his future he could brightly see.

Dive In

The water that my eyes did meet
Was cool and crisp as icy sleet.
And so I ran with fervent might
To enjoy in expectant delight.
With towel in hand and trunks on fleek
I knew this swim wasnt for the meek.
I climbed the steps up onto the deck
With the temperature of the water to check.
So I dipped my toes into the pool
And soon realized it was too cool.
As chills were sent up my spine,
I understood the choice was mine.
And so I retreated in ghastly fright,
For fear of getting frostbite.
But soon I went and tried once more
To test the water as I did before.
As I quivered and hestitantly went,
I dipped my toe with anxious intent.
Another chill went through me then,
And I retreated back yet again.
How could I do this polar plunge,
Lest I run and take the lunge.
And so I stood in defeated thought
Of whether I stood jump in or not.
But my lesson I hope you learn is this,

Will you take leap or will you miss?
The choice is yours and really quite plain,
Will you go for your dreams or live in vain?

Butterfly Destiny

Take a butterfly, a symbol of beauty and change,
But look how it started, a caterpillar that was
strange.
An insect that was destined for more,
It didnt know what was in store.
For if we knew of the day we would fly,
We wouldnt be so sad when our old selves die.
For change to happen, we must always know,
That it doesnt just happen, and that it can be
slow.
Right now we may not see the beauty ahead,
But one day we'll have wings to spread.
The fear isnt in failure and strife,
Its in flying in this beautiful life.
Right now we may feel stuck and not right,
But soon we'll have wings so we can take flight.
Dont worry about where you are just now,
Ans the darkness that ensues you cant allow.
Things may seem ugly and not make sense,
But soon you'll be able to soar above that fence.
The beauty inside you will one day shine,
And the story of pain you can redefine.

Listen

When i try and explain how i feel,
I'm not looking for words that heal,
Im looking for ears that can hear,
And try to understand my fear.
I don't need words that I've heard before,
Im looking for someone to listen more.
Let me explain the pain im in,
And give me ears that'll just listen.
I'm not doing ok as i feel right now,
And I know that I'll make it somehow.
So hold me tight, in arms or in thought,
So i can feel the love that ive often sought.
Listen to the sound of the tears i cry,
And let me know youre not going to pass me by.
I cant always explain the way that I feel,
But i want you to know that this pain is real.
Im not making it up and it wont just pass,
I often feel that i'll break like glass.
Handle me with care as I go through this mess,
And know that its real unlike Lochness.
I cant always deal with all my feelings inside,
So sometimes I retreat and go off and hide.
I cry and I sleep and i wonder why me,
But mostly I struggle just to be.
So handle me with care, im easily hurt,

Just listen to my words and dont throw dirt.
I often wont say im feel sad and down,
Because i dont want to burden you with my
frown.
So just let me know youre there when i need
you,
And let me process the pain as i need to.
I cant just be happy, trust me ive tried,
Some days i feel like part of me died.
You want me to see that its going to be fine,
But its not always so easy to see that line.
Im trying to do better and im tired of this pain,
It feels like im drowning when there is no rain.
Your words dont always help, im sorry to say,
Just let me know youre there and going to stay.
Im know its not easy to see me this way,
But you must know its only for a day.
So handle me with care and others alike,
Our mood often changes and goes on strike.
Just listen to the pain that cannot be said,
And listen to the silence that cant be read.
Handle with care,
And just be there.

Set Free

You're only human, and i want you to know,
Its ok to stumble and sometimes move slow.
You weren't meant to be prefect, so understand
this,
Your purpose and meaning you did not miss.
Life can be hard and its often not fun,
To stumble and fall when you've only begun.
You weren't meant to be perfect, but this Ive
known,
Just take a look at at just how far you have
grown.
You've fallen before and you rose from the
ground,
So why now do you doubt that you can rebound?
You weren't meant to be perfect, surely you
know,
But from this turmoil you'll undoubtably grow.
Its ok to faulter and stumble and fall,
But one day soon you stand again tall.
Don't let this thing kill you or bring about doubt,
One day you'll look back and see what this pain
was about.
You weren't meant to be perfect, but this you can
see,
Now isn't forever, and soon you'll be set free.

Hold On

Just a Little Bit Longer

When you want to give up and throw it away,
And you've taken all you can bare for just one
day.
When your hand has cramped and you cant last
much longer,
I want you to know youre so much stronger.
Youre stronger than you think and smarter than
you know,
Each battle you fight helps your strength grow.
So hold on my warrior, its not over yet,
You'll make it through somehow, i'm willing to
bet.
When youre tired and weary and you cant feel
your hand,
Just remember that you can always stand.
Stand on His promise of victory and hope,
But dont lose yourself when you begin to mope.
It all seems bleak and the dark has ensued,
But I promise its just your vision that has been
skewed.
If you remeber one thing, my dearest friend,
It's to hold on till the very end.
Be of good courage and keep pressing through,

Just hold on a little bit longer, yes you.

Anxious Thoughts

When you're anxiety is high and you can't calm
down,
Stop what you're doing and pretend you have on
a crown.
Stand tall with purpose and firm with poise,
And turn off all of the outside noise.
Breathe deeply in and hold just for a moment,
And enlist in yourself for this enrollment.
Expand your lungs and fill up with ease,
And exhale all of the negative please.
Repeat slowly for a count of five,
Inhale and exhale, you're going to survive.
When anxiety comes knocking on your door,
It simply means you're not in balance anymore.
So take a step back and stand up tall,
And breathe in and out, give it your all.
For this moment in time simply focus on you,
And follow your breath as you bring yourself to.
Breathe in good thoughts and breathe out bad,
And don't focus on what has been making you
sad.
This does take practice but I promise in due
time,
You'll be feeling at peace if you remember this
rhyme.

Ripple Effect

To all the world forgotten.
A whisper in the wind.
A shadow of someone they once knew,
but cant remember how.
To most I never existed.
Never a stranger that passed them by.
To some a faceless memory.
To others a bitter taste
in their pursuit of happiness.
The world wouldnt remember me
except a few photographs
of a once farmiliar face,
but now a distant memory.
Merely a shadow in the background
of someone's life.
I never truly existed.
Simply passed by on my way.
No one remembers.
I left no legacy behind.
Just a mere short ripple
in the waves of an endless ocean.

Dark Days

I remember how the sun
would gently kiss my face
with its warmth and beauty.
I remember how it felt to play in the sun
and how bright it was.
But now all I feel
is the piercing cold of darkness
as it engulphs my dreams.
The howling wind that carries
all that I once enjoyed
into the endless abyss
that now haunts my nightmares.
The sun feels like a forgotten dream;
a dream that children have
before they awaken
to the harsh realities of life.
I've forgotten what life used to be like,
for the endless bitter cold
stretches on for a lifetime of its own.

Broken

I'm broken, I'm shattered, my life is in pieces,
Every time I look, the number increases.
I've been punched and gutted and I dont know
how,
But I've survived all that and made it to right
now.
I tried so hard to remain strong and brave,
But I ended up hiding inside my cave.
There I met only darkness, and greeted with
ease,
For the light I tried to shine was only a tease.
When youre broken and down you stop caring
so much,
You forget what it means to have that gentle soft
touch.
This life will break you, leave you shattered and
torn,
But you must pick up the pieces if you want to
be reborn.
How, you ask, can I get through this life,
And get through this torment and terrible strife?
There is only One who can transform your
sorrow,
And give you a life you never could borrow.
One to strength to make you anew,

And create something from nothing and carry
you through.
Jehovah Rapha, the Lord who heals and restores,
I pray you find Him and make Him personally
yours.

Rise Up

As the sun sets today,
filling the sky
with an array of beautiful, vibrant colors,
I felt a sense of peace.
As the sun laid its head to rest,
I knew that it would rise again tomorrow.
For each day,
I saw the sun go down,
only to rise again the next day.
Every day,
without fail
and without anyone needing to tell it to,
the sun rises.
And because of this,
I know that I too
shall rise again when I fall.
I too,
shall get back up
when the darkness of life
seems to have all but consumed me.
I know that tomorrow the sun shall rise,
and I shall rise with it.

My Legacy

As Ariel lived her days on land as a mute,
I feel as though my voice goes unheard.
Unnoticed by people as they pass on by,
I feel like the chameleon
who blends in to the background.
I had a voice;
at least I think I did.
I had an opinion,
a voiced concern,
but now my voice is gone.
I no longer speak,
for there are no ears to listen.
So I write my words down,
in hopes that some day
someone will find them
and will hear what it is I have to say.
Someday my words can penetrate
the endless chatter about nothing
and someone will hear my small voice.
Maybe someday others
who have lived their life on mute
will finally get a chance to say
the words they've been holding in,
ready to burst forth
and create a new world

or at least a new world around them.
Maybe someday those who have suffered
in slience will suffer no more.
Maybe someday people will learn to listen
to those crying for help,
unable to speak up
or afraid of what others may say.
One day, I hope my words are known
about a little boy who just wanted
to be seen and heard.

Transformed

Secrets kept and truth untold
Oh how I've watched my troubles unfold
Silence known and words unspoken
I've tried so hard to stay unbroken
Held together with lies and deception
Suffering in silence from depression
Always drowning and never seen
I've never known a true shoulder to lean
Always changing to exceptation
Never seeing that limitation
Journies end and memories lost
I never realized the ultimate cost
My life in shambles and pieces gone
Always feeling like someone's pawn
But healing hurts and is a bloody mess
But hope is found when you fear less
The old me now is dead and gone
New life begins like a new dawn
Don't mourn the past misconception
See what's new with divine perception